Month-by-Month Poetry
March, April, May, June

Compiled by Marian Reiner

SCHOLASTIC
PROFESSIONAL BOOKS

NEW YORK • TORONTO • LONDON • AUCKLAND • SYDNEY
MEXICO CITY • NEW DELHI • HONG KONG

For Eleri, Sydney, and Sterling—
our adored spring flowers

Cover design by Jaime Lucero
Cover illustration by Amanda Haley
Interior design by Solutions by Design, Inc.
Interior illustration James Graham Hale

ISBN: 0-590-37903-8

We gratefully acknowledge permission to reprint the following selections:

"Butterfly Song" from *Music of the Acoma, Isleta, Cochiti and Zuni Pueblos*. Bureau of American Ethnology Bulletin 165 by Frances Densmore, Smithsonian Institution, Washington, D.C. 1957, p. 38.

"Puddles" and "Tree" from *Country Pie* by Frank Asch. Text copyright © 1979 by Frank Asch. Reprinted by permission of Greenwillow Books, a division of William Morrow & Company, Inc.

"Flowers" from *Windy Morning* by Harry Behn. Copyright © 1953 Harry Behn. © renewed 1981 by Alice Behn Goebel, Pamela Behn Adam, Prescott Behn and Peter Behn. Used by permission of Marian Reiner.

"Jumping Rope" from *Playtime in the City* by Lee Blair, published by Garrard Publishing, 1971. Used by permission of Dr. Allan D. Jacobs.

"The Rainbow" from *Collected Poems* by Iain Crichton-Smith. By permission of Carcanet Press Limited.

"Letter to Bee" from *The Poems of Emily Dickinson*, Thomas H. Johnson, ed., Cambridge, MA: The Belknap Press of Harvard University Press, Copyright © 1951, 1955, 1979, 1983 by the President and Fellows of Harvard College. Reprinted by permission of the publishers and the Trustees of Amherst College.

"On Mother's Day" from *Skip Around the Year* by Aileen Fisher. Copyright © 1967 Aileen Fisher. Renewed © 1995 Aileen Fisher. "Baby Chick" from *Runny Days, Sunny Days* by Aileen Fisher. Copyright © 1958, 1986 Aileen Fisher. "June" from *Going Barefoot* by Aileen Fisher. Copyright © 1960 Aileen Fisher. Renewed © 1988 Aileen Fisher. "Seeds" by Aileen Fisher appeared first in *The Weekly Reader*. Copyright © 1954 Aileen Fisher. "Wearing of the Green" from *Holiday Poems for Boys and Girls*, Plays Inc. Copyright © 1956 Aileen Fisher. All are reprinted by permission of Marian Reiner for the author.

"Tree's Place" from *Old Elm Speaks* by Kristine O'Connell George. Text copyright © 1998 Kristine O'Connell George. Reprinted by permission of Clarion Books, a Houghton Mifflin Company imprint.

"The Winner" and "April" by Patricia Hubbell. Copyright © 1999 by Patricia Hubbell. Used by permission of Marian Reiner for the author.

"The Lesson" by Jane W. Krows form *The Sound of Poetry* edited by Mary C. Austin and Queenie Mills. Published 1964 by Allyn and Bacon, Inc. Extensive research failed to find the copyright holder of this work.

"Spring Fling" by Monica Kulling originally appeared in *Cricket*. Copyright © 1993 Monica Kulling. "March," "hot shot" and "Sidewalk Singer" are copyright © 1999 by Monica Kulling. All are used by permission of Marian Reiner for the author.

"For Father's Day" by Sandra Liatsos. Copyright © 1992 by Sandra Liatsos. "Rain" by Sandra Liatsos. Copyright © 1981 by Sandra Liatsos. "Spring in the Woods" by Sandra Liatsos. Copyright © 1989 by Sandra Liatsos. "Green Crayon" by Sandra Liatsos. Copyright © 1999 by Sandra Liatsos. All are reprinted by permission of Marian Reiner for the author.

"The Balloon Man" from *Whispers and Other Poems* by Myra Cohn Livingston. Copyright © 1958 Myra Cohn Livingston. Renewed © 1986 Myra Cohn Livingston. Used by permission of Marian Reiner.

"A Yell for Yellow" from *There Is No Rhyme for Silver* by Eve Merriam. Copyright © 1962, 1990 Eve Merriam. Used by permission of Marian Reiner.

"Little Seeds We Sow in Spring" by Else Holmelund Minarik. Text copyright © 1964 by Else Holmelund Minarik. Used by permission of HarperCollins Publishers.

"Hey, Bug!" from *I Feel the Same Way* by Lilian Moore. Copyright © 1967, 1995 Lilian Moore. Reprinted by permission of Marian Reiner for the author.

"Wind Pictures" from *Winds* by Mary O'Neill. Copyright © 1970 by Mary O'Neill. Renewed © 1998 Abigail Hagler and Erin Baroni. Used by permission of Marian Reiner.

"Flowers Are a Silly Bunch" from *Once Upon a Horse* by Arnold Spilka. Copyright © 1966 Arnold Spilka. Renewed © 1994 Arnold Spilka. Used by permission of the author.

"Listen!," "Garden Gals" and "Being a Kite" by Jacqueline Sweeney. Copyright © 1999 by Jacqueline Sweeney. Used by permission of Marian Reiner for the author.

"Rainy Day" by Gina Bell-Zano, "Beetles in the Garden" by Elsie S. Lindgren, "Smells of Summer" by Vivan Gouled, "June Fourteenth" by Winifred C. Marshall and "School" by Iva Riebel Judy are from *Poetry Place Anthology*. Copyright © 1983 Edgell Communications, Inc. Used by permission of Scholastic, Inc.

"Baby Animals" by Meish Goldish from *Animals Poems from A to Z* (Scholastic, 1996). "Ladybug Rhyme" by Maria Fleming from *Big Poetry Animals* copyright © 1996 Maria Fleming. "Frog Song" by Liza Charlesworth from *Big Poetry Animals* copyright © 1996 Liza Charlesworth. All are by permission of Scholastic Professional Books and authors.

Contents

May

June

Introduction

Welcome to *Month-by-Month Poetry: March, April, May, June*. This seasonal collection contains more than 60 poems for use in the classroom—poems selected to engage your students, build literacy, and celebrate the coming of spring.

With spring comes new growth. What better way to foster growth in your students than to share poetry with them? Poetry captures the essence of life experiences. It clarifies thoughts, deepens understanding, and brings meaning, wisdom, and beauty to light. Poetry strengthens skills in reading, speaking, and listening. It teaches phonics by example and serves as a springboard for activities in math, science, language arts, and all other areas of the curriculum.

Use this book as a tool to help bring the enchantment of poetry to your students. The poems in this collection are fun and easy to read. They explore spring topics from March winds to the last days of school. You'll find verses on trees and flowers, kites, caterpillars, and more. For easy reference, we've divided the poems by month. March poems relate to clouds, spring winds, and the color green. April poems feature rainy days and shadows. May poems move to butterflies and flowers, while poems for June cover gardens, baby animals, and frogs.

The following activities offer some ideas for using the poems in your classroom. Use them across the curriculum and help your students learn while developing a love and appreciation for poetry. Read poetry aloud and often. Sprinkle it around your classroom and in all subject areas. Make your classroom a poetry zone, where all are encouraged to seek and enjoy the pleasures of poetry.

Spring Fling!
open the windows
swing wide the doors
roll up the carpet
dance on the floors

unshut the house
that stuffy old thing
let in the light!
let in the spring!

take off the roof
shout to the sky
it feels like spring
and so do I!
    —Monica Kulling

Activities Ideas

MAKE A POETRY POSTER

Copy the words of a poem on a large sheet of poster board. Invite students, one or two at a time, to come up to the poster and draw a small picture near the poem. Hang the decorated poster in the hallway, on your classroom door, or on a wall in your classroom. Some poems that prompt creative illustrations are "Green Crayon," "A Yell for Yellow," and "Flowers."

ELECT A POEM OF THE WEEK

Share several poems with your students, and ask them to vote on which one should be "Poem of the Week." Write the chosen poem on chart paper, and hang it on display. Then make the poem a guest of honor in your classroom with a week's worth of special activities surrounding it. Some suggested activities include:

- **Read-aloud day.** Read the poem aloud as a class. Let students take turns reading aloud dialogue in the poem "The Winner."

- **Expand on details in the poem.** Ask your students to pretend they are lilies pushing up through the earth or birds building nests in the poem "May Song." Have them write about their experiences. Mount their work on construction paper cut in the shape of flowers, birds' nests, or other details in the poem.

- **Use lines from the poem as captions.** Ask each child to choose a line from the poem and draw a picture to go with it. On its own, each line of poetry can serve as a caption.

- **Imitate the poem.** After a week's worth of exposure to the poem, invite your students to write their own in imitation of the "Poem of the Week."

GET UP AND GO!

Share poems that inspire movement in your classroom. Poems such as "Spring Wind" and "Being a Kite" describe movements your students can imitate. Read each poem several times through. Then read it again, urging your students to stand up and move with the verses.

ADD COLOR TO YOUR DAY

Bring colors alive in the classroom by sharing poems that mention or rely on colors. "Green Crayon" and "A Yell for Yellow" focus on single colors. After reading one of these poems, you might have your students color a picture entirely in green or in yellow, write a note to a family member in green or yellow colored pencil, or draw pictures of things that are green or yellow (other than those things mentioned in the poem). "I'm Glad the Sky Is Painted Blue" suggests a peaceful scene emerging. Ask students to color a blue strip across the top of a white piece of paper and a green strip at the bottom. Then urge them to draw their own ideas of what's sandwiched in between.

USE POEMS IN POCKET CHARTS

Write each line of a poem on a separate strip of tagboard. Place the lines in order in the pocket chart, and read the poem aloud. Then use the poem in different ways:

- **Keep a rhyme in your pocket.** Put a rhyming poem in your pocket chart to emphasize and reinforce the use of rhyme. Invite students to come up and point out the words that rhyme.

- **Sort rhyming words.** Write the poem on chart paper. With students' help, underline words that rhyme (such as <u>say</u> and <u>Day</u> in the poem *April Fool's Day*). Write each rhyming pair on an index card, and place it on the far left side of the pocket chart. Invite the children to think of words that rhyme with each pair. Write these on index cards, and place them in rows alongside the appropriate pairs. Your chart might look like this:

RHYMING WORDS

say	day	jay	pay
so	know	hoe	bow

Rhyming poems useful for this activity include "My Shadow," "On Mother's Day," "Seeds," and "What Do You Suppose?"

- **Add pictures to poetry.** Place the title of the poem in the top pocket and the first line of the poem in the second pocket. Then continue down the chart, skipping one pocket between lines. Provide squares of tagboard, and invite students to draw pictures to go with specific words in the poem (such as *cat, mouse,* and *worms* from the poem "Rain"). Assign words to eliminate repetition. Read the poem aloud. When you reach a word that names one of the drawings, have the student place his/her drawing on the pocket chart, just below the appropriate line of the poem. Then read the poem again, with illustrations in place. Short poems, such as "Rain" and "Butterfly Song," work best.

SPRING INTO SPRING!

Devote time to sharing poems specifically about the coming of spring. After sharing the poems, ask students to write their own poems about spring's coming and what that means to them. "Spring Fling!" and "Spring in the Woods" provide strong examples of springtime excitement.

SAVOR THE SOUNDS OF POETRY

Read aloud the poem "Listen!" Invite students to talk about the sounds they hear in the poem. Provide paper, and encourage students to work in small groups to imitate the poem, describing sounds of the classroom, sounds of the summer, or other sounds in detail. Younger students may want to describe sounds by speaking rather than writing.

MORE AND MORE METAPHOR!

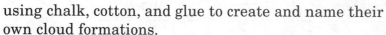

Explore the use of metaphor in poetry. Have students draw the images conveyed in poems that use metaphor, such as "March" and "Wind Pictures." For example, they might illustrate "Wind Pictures" by

using chalk, cotton, and glue to create and name their own cloud formations.

REACH FOR THE RAIN

Celebrate the wetness of spring with a rain date in your classroom. Prior to the special day, find and photocopy all the rain-, water-, or puddle-related poems in this book. Assign each student or pair of students one of the poems to read aloud in class on the special rain date. Let them practice their poems for several days. On the appointed day, have students bring in raincoats, boots, and other raingear from home. (Watch out for umbrellas, though, as these can cause injury.) Have students don their raingear and let the reading begin! Poems especially appropriate for reading include "Listen!" and "What the Rain Said."

CHANGE THE SHAPE OF POEMS

Share with students the poem "Tree's Place." Invite them to tell what is special about the poem—its unique shape! Let students write their own poetry in the shape of its content or convert existing poems into different shapes. Poems in this book that can be shape-converted include "The Balloon Man," "hot shot," and "Beetles in the Garden."

I WISH I COULD BE...

Let students imitate the poets who envisioned themselves as trees, kites, and other spring-related objects. Share with your students poems that express the idea "I wish I could be..." These include "Tree," "A Kite," "Being a Kite," and "Hot Shot." Let your students depart from the poem and write or draw themselves *being* one of these items. What would it feel like to be a tree? Would they be a young tree or an old tree? Short or tall? How high would they fly as a kite? What would they see in the air?

COUNT ON IT!

Help your students make math out of poetry. Read a poem, such as "Rain," "Jumping Rope," and "The Chickens." Have students count the animals in the poem and write math sums or word problems based on the details. For example, in "Rain," students can

- ◎ count six animal names mentioned.

- ◎ make word problems, such as "1 dog plus 1 cat = 2 pets."

- ◎ draw the animal sets showing their own number of birds or worms, as these are not numbered in the poem.

CREATE COMIC STRIPS

Let poems be a springboard for inventiveness with the creation of comic strips based on the theme or content of a poem. Children can draw their own comic strips to re-tell the story described in "Hey, Bug!," reveal the big news in "The Secret," and tell a funny joke in "Frog."

SOLVE PUZZLING POEMS

How long will it take your students to decode the witty "Autograph Verse"? Young readers may need help. Older students will enjoy the challenge of being the first to discover reading up and down. After solving this one, students may enjoy creating their own puzzling poems, independently or in small groups. If there's enough interest, compile student puzzles to make a class puzzle book. Reproduce enough books for all students in your class to have their own.

March

spring is a lion
pacing its cage
restless and roaring
and storming with rage

spring is a lamb
under a tree
feeding or sleeping
as calm as can be

Monica Kulling

The Winner

"I'm best!" said Rain,
  "I'm best!" said Snow,
"I'm warm," said Rain,
  "I'm cold," said Snow,
"I slosh," said Rain,
  "I slide," said Snow,
"*I shine*," said Sun, "*and away you both go!*"

Patricia Hubbell

Month-by-Month Poetry: March, April, May, June Scholastic Professional Books, 1999

Listen!

The rain

hits the puddles
pop-pop-plop

pings the roof
spat-a-tat-tat

zaps the sidewalks
sizzily-pizzily

slaps the ground
woppity-thud

smoozily-oozily
squooshes to mud.

Jacqueline Sweeney

What the Rain Said

"Splash," said a raindrop
   As it fell upon my hat:
"Splash," said another
   As it trickled down my back.
"You are very rude, " I said
   As I looked up to the sky:
Then *another* raindrop splashed
   Right into my eye!

Anonymous

One Misty, Moisty Morning

One misty, moisty morning,
   When cloudy was the weather,
I chanced to meet an old man,
   Clothed all in leather.
He began to compliment
   And I began to grin.
How do you do? And how do you do?
   And how do you do again?

   Anonymous

Spring Fling!

open the windows
swing wide the doors
roll up the carpet
dance on the floors

unshut the house
that stuffy old thing
let in the light!
let in the spring!

take off the roof
shout to the sky
it feels like spring
and so do I!

Monica Kulling

Month-by-Month Poetry: March, April, May, June Scholastic Professional Books, 1999

Never Mind, March

Never mind, March, we know
When you blow
You're not really mad
Or angry or bad;
You're only blowing the winter away
To get the world ready for April and May.

Unknown

Spring Wind

I come to work as well as play;
    I'll tell you what I do;
I whistle all the live-long day,
    "Woo-oo-oo-oo! Woo-oo!"

I toss the branches up and down
    And shake them to and fro,
I whirl the leaves in flocks of brown,
    And send them high and low.

I strew the twigs upon the ground,
    The frozen earth I sweep;
I blow the children round and round
    And wake the flowers from sleep.

Anonymous

Wind Pictures

Look! There's a giant stretching in the sky,
A thousand white-maned horses flying by,
A house, a mother mountain with her hills,
A lazy lady posing in her frills,
Cotton floating from a thousand bales,
And a white ship with white sails.

See the old witch fumbling with her shawl,
White towers piling on a castle wall,
The bits of soft that break and fall away,
Air-borne mushrooms with undersides of gray—
Above, a white doe races with her fawn
On the white grass of a celestial lawn.
Lift up your lovely heads and look
As wind turns clouds into a picture book.

Mary O'Neill

Wearing of the Green

It ought to come in April,
or, better yet, in May
when everything is green as green—
I mean St. Patrick's Day.

With still a week of winter
this wearing of the green
seems rather out of season—
it's rushing things, I mean.

But maybe March *is* better
when all is done and said:
St. Patrick brings a promise,
a four-leaf-clover promise,
a green-all-over promise
of springtime just ahead!

Aileen Fisher

Little Elf-Man

I met a little elf-man, once,
Down where the lillies blow.
I asked him why he was so small,
And why he didn't grow.

He slightly frowned, and with his eye
He looked me through and through.
"I'm quite as big for me," said he,
"As you are big for you."

John Kendrick Bangs

Month-by-Month Poetry: March, April, May, June Scholastic Professional Books, 1999

The Balloon Man

The balloon man's stall
Is near the wall.

And in the Spring
There's not a thing
In the afternoon
Like a bright balloon.

(Big ones or small
Round as a ball,
Balloons with a string
Or with nothing at all.)

He stands near the wall
In his bright-colored stall
And sells balloons
In the afternoons
In the Spring.

Myra Cohn Livingston

Green Crayon

My crayon flies
across the space
and makes it grow
green flowers, trees,
green children each
with a bright green face.
I won't use pink,
or red or yellow,
orange, brown or blue
because I've lost them—
all but green.
I'm glad
the winter's through.

Sandra Liatsos

Month-by-Month Poetry: March, April, May, June Scholastic Professional Books, 1999

Spring in the Woods

Wake up, woodchuck!
  Wake up bear!
Stretch and yawn
  in April air.
Come outside.
  Prowl and play.
Spring is everywhere—
  TODAY!

Sandra Liatsos

April

Buds begin. The crocus glows.
Bears throw off their winter doze.
Water flows and flows and flows.
My winter boots forget my toes.

Patricia Hubbell

April Fools' Day

The first of April, some do say,
Is set aside for All Fools' Day,
But why the people call it so
Nor I nor they themselves do know.

Anonymous

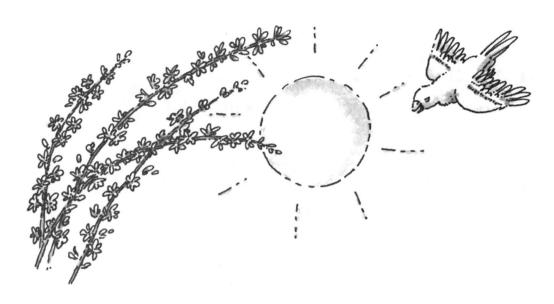

A Yell for Yellow

Yellow, yellow, hello, yellow:
Welcome to forsythia and dandelions in Spring,
To buttercups and goldenrod and warblers on the wing.

Yellow, yellow, mellow yellow:
Yellow as new wood, yellow as wheat,
Yellow as cornbread sweet to eat.

Yellow, Yellow, let's bellow yellow:
Yellow monkeys peeling bananas!
Yellow chickens playing pianos!
Butterflies, goldfish, cats' eyes!

Yellow, yellow, yell on yellow:
Yellow is a lemon smell, it tingles like a sneeze,
Tickles like the sunshine, jingles like a breeze!

Eve Merriam

Tree's Place

Tree has staked its claim,
anchoring itself firmly to Earth.
Tree owns this place in the universe.
Within this space, all belongs to Tree—
turf, shaft of air, even slices of sun.
Tree will not step aside for anyone.
Tree stands its ground.
When you
meet Tree,
you *must*
go around.

Kristine O'Connell George

Month-by-Month Poetry: March, April, May, June Scholastic Professional Books, 1999

A Kite

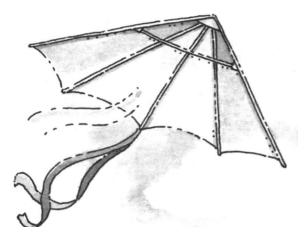

I often sit and wish that I
Could be a kite up in the sky,
And ride upon the breeze and go
Whichever way I chanced to blow.

Anonymous

Tree

If only I could stand
still enough, long enough,
with my arms in the air,
I'm sure I could become
a tree.
After a while my fingers would turn green
and my toes would turn down into the ground.
Every day I'd drink the sunlight
and taste the earth,
but then one day I'd scream,
"Hey, it's me!"
and I'd tell everyone
just what it was like to be
a tree.

Frank Asch

Being a Kite

If I were a kite
I'd kneel,
stretch my skinny arms
out wide,
and wait for wind.

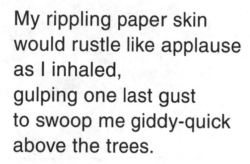

My yellow shirt would
fill up like a sail
and flap,
tugging my criss-crossed
wooden bones and me
towards seas of cloud.

My rippling paper skin
would rustle like applause
as I inhaled,
gulping one last gust
to swoop me giddy-quick
above the trees.

My red rag tail
would drift
toward everything green
to balance me

so all day
  I could
    loop and climb

  loop and climb

     and
     soar
into pure sky.

Jacqueline Sweeney

Month-by-Month Poetry: March, April, May, June Scholastic Professional Books, 1999

Rain

The cat is peeking from the door.
The dog has hurried to his house.
The birds are huddled in the trees.
I see no furry mole nor mouse.
The only ones outdoors with me
To celebrate the April rain
Are worms who wriggle with delight
To be in silver streams again.

Sandra Liatsos

Puddles

I like to look in puddles—
when I smile
they smile,
when I laugh
they laugh,
and when I cry
they don't mind getting wet.

Frank Asch

Month-by-Month Poetry: March, April, May, June Scholastic Professional Books, 1999

Rainy Day

I used to hate a rainy day.
There were no outside games to play,
And even though our house was roomy
The gray rain made the inside gloomy.
Now, I don't mind the rain at all,
For when no friends come to call,
I've all the company I need.
I pick me out a book, and read!

Gina Bell-Zano

Month-by-Month Poetry: March, April, May, June Scholastic Professional Books, 1999

Sidewalk Singer

I glide
on my roller blades
all day long
I'm swift
and sure
I weave
and whirr
At night
with my skates off
I feel the beat
The sidewalk singing
in my feet

Monica Kulling

My Shadow

I have a little shadow
   That goes in and out with me.
And what can be the use of him
   Is more than I can see!
He is very, very like me
   From the heels up to the head;
And I see him jump before me,
   When I jump into my bed.

Robert Louis Stevenson

Month-by-Month Poetry: March, April, May, June Scholastic Professional Books, 1999

Jumping Rope

See!
See!
See!
I'm jumping rope!
I'll jump
Fifty times
I hope!
I've jumped
Ten times.
I've jumped twenty.
I've jumped
Thirty times.
That's plenty!

Lee Blair

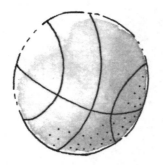

Hot Shot

I am the basketball
after I throw it

arcing mighty
in a clean, high
sweep

making mouths
hang open

Monica Kulling

Month-by-Month Poetry: March, April, May, June   Scholastic Professional Books, 1999

The Swing

How do you like to go up in a swing,
    Up in the air so blue?
Oh, I do think it the pleasantest thing
    Ever a child can do!

Up in the air and over the wall,
    Till I can see so wide,
Rivers and trees and cattle and all
    Over the countryside—

Till I look down on the garden green,
    Down on the roof so brown—
Up in the air I go flying again,
    Up in the air and down!

Robert Louis Stevenson

May-Time

There is but one May in the year,
    And sometimes May is wet and cold;
There is but one May in the year,
    But before the year grows old.

Yet, though it be the chilliest May
    With least of sun, and most of showers,
Its wind and dew, its night and day,
    Bring up the flowers.

Anonymous

Month-by-Month Poetry: March, April, May, June Scholastic Professional Books, 1999

May Song

Spring is coming, spring is coming,
   Birdies, build your nest;
Weave together straw and feather,
   Doing each your best.

Spring is coming, spring is coming,
   Flowers are coming too;
Pansies, lilies, daffodillies,
   Now are coming through.

Spring is coming, spring is coming,
   All around is fair;
Shimmer and quiver on the river,
   Joy is everywhere.

   Old English Country Rhyme

On Mother's Day

On Mother's Day we got up first,
so full of plans we almost burst.

We started breakfast right away
as our surprise for Mother's Day.

We picked some flowers, then hurried back
to make the coffee—rather black.

We wrapped our gifts and wrote a card
and boiled the eggs—a little hard.

And then we sang a serenade,
which burned the toast, I am afraid.

But Mother said, amidst our cheers,
"Oh, what a big surprise, my dears.
I've not had such a treat in years."
And she was smiling to her ears!

Aileen Fisher

Butterfly Song

Butterfly, butterfly, butterfly, butterfly,
Oh, look, see it hovering among the flowers!
It is like a baby trying to walk and not knowing how to go.
The clouds sprinkle down the rain.

Acoma Indian song, translated by Frances Densmore

La Mariposa Linda

Ayer que fuimos al campo.
Vi una linda mariposa.

Pero ella, al verme tan cerca,
Voló y voló presurosa.

The Pretty Butterfly

Yesterday I went to the field.
I saw a beautiful butterfly.

But on seeing me so close,
It flew away ever so quickly.

Hispanic Nursery Rhyme

I'm Glad the Sky Is Painted Blue

I'm glad the sky is painted blue,
  And the earth is painted green,
With such a lot of nice fresh air
  All sandwiched in between.

Anonymous

Seeds

Seeds know just the way to start—
I wonder how they get so smart.

They *could* come up in garden beds
feet first—by standing on their heads.

They *could* forget if they should grow
like sunflowers, high, or pumpkins, low.

They *could* forget their colors, too,
and yet they never, never do.

Aileen Fisher

Month-by-Month Poetry: March, April, May, June Scholastic Professional Books, 1999

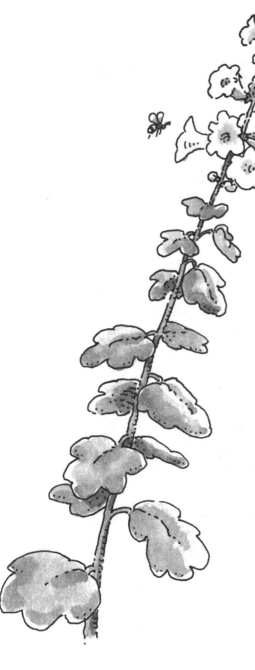

Flowers

We planted a garden
Of all kinds of flowers
And it grew very well
Because there were showers,
And the bees came and buzzed:
This garden is ours!

But every day
To the honeyed bowers
The butterflies come
And hover for hours
Over the daisies
And hollyhock towers.

So we let the honey
Be theirs, but the flowers
We cut to take
In the house are ours,
Not yours, if you please,
You busy bees!

Harry Behn

Little Seeds We Sow in Spring

Little seeds we sow in spring
growing while the robins sing,
give us carrots, peas and beans,
tomatoes, pumpkins, squash and greens.

And we pick them,
one and all,
through the summer,
through the fall.

Winter comes, then spring, and then
little seeds we sow again.

Else Holmelund Minarik

Do You Carrot All for Me?

Do you carrot all for me?
My heart beets for you,
With your turnip nose
And your radish face,
You are a peach.
If we cantaloupe,
Lettuce marry:
Weed make a swell pear.

Anonymous

Beetles in the Garden

Beetles
may be
large or small,
shaped from
flat to
humpy tall,
iridescent,
red or
yellow—
every one
is a hungry fellow.

Elsie S. Lindgren

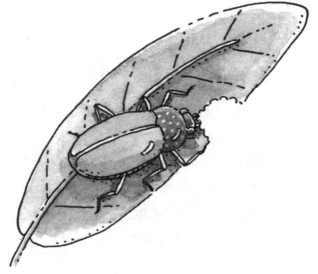

Ladybug Rhyme

Ladybugs all dressed in red
Strolling through the flower bed—
If I were tiny just like you,
I'd creep among the flowers, too

Maria Fleming

Letter to Bee

Bee! I'm expecting you!
Was saying Yesterday
To Somebody you know
That you were due—

The Frogs got Home last Week—
Are settled, and at work—
Birds, mostly back—
The Clover warm and thick—

You'll get my Letter by
The seventeenth; Reply
Or better, be with me—
Yours, Fly.

Emily Dickinson

What Do You Suppose?

What do you suppose?
A bee sat on my nose.
Then what do you think?
He gave me a wink
And said, "I beg your pardon,
I thought you were the garden."

Anonymous

Hey, Bug!

Hey, bug, stay!
Don't run away.
I know a game that we can play.

I'll hold my fingers very still
and you can climb a finger-hill.

No, no.
Don't go.

Here's a wall—a tower, too,
a tiny bug town, just for you.
I've a cookie. You have some.
Take this oatmeal cookie crumb.

Hey, bug, stay!
Hey, bug!
Hey!

Lilian Moore

Caterpillar

Brown and furry
Caterpillar in a hurry,
Take your walk
To the shady leaf, or stalk,
Or what not,
Which may be the chosen spot.
No toad spy you,
Hovering bird of prey pass by you;
Spin and die,
To live again a butterfly.

Christina Rossetti

June

The day is warm
and a breeze is blowing,
the sky is blue
and its eye is glowing,
and everything's new
and green and growing...

My shoes are off
and my socks are showing...

My socks are off...

do you know how I'm going?

BAREFOOT!

Aileen Fisher

Month-by-Month Poetry: March, April, May, June Scholastic Professional Books, 1999

In the Garden

Went to the garden
Picked up a pin
Asked who was out
Asked who was in.
Nobody in
Nobody out
Down in the garden
Walking about.

Anonymous

Garden Gals

Lazy Susan
Holly, Daisy
Fern, Petunia
Iris, Pansy

Ladies' names
in gardens grow,
but which came first
do you suppose

the lily
    or
Aunt Rose?

Jacqueline Sweeney

Flowers Are a Silly Bunch

Flowers are a silly bunch
While trees are sort of bossy.
Lakes are shy
The earth is calm
And rivers do seem saucy.
Hills are good
But mountains mean
While weeds all ask for pity.
I guess the country can be nice
But I live in the city.

Arnold Spilka

Month-by-Month Poetry: March, April, May, June Scholastic Professional Books, 1999

The Secret

We have a secret, just we three,
The robin and I, and the sweet cherry-tree;
The bird told the tree, and the tree told me,
And nobody knows it but just us three.

But of course the robin knows it best,
Because she built the—I shan't tell the rest;
And laid the four little—something in it—
I'm afraid I shall tell it every minute.

But if the tree and the robin don't peep,
I'll try my best the secret to keep;
Though I know when the little birds fly about
Then the whole secret will be out.

Anonymous

June Fourteenth

Can you tell why we celebrate
   This very special day,
And have you noticed waving flags
   All up and down the way?

The bands will play, the children march,
   And all the crowds will cheer.
It is the birthday of our flag,
   A day that we hold dear.

Winifred C. Marshall

Month-by-Month Poetry: March, April, May, June   Scholastic Professional Books, 1999

For Father's Day

I found a seashell
for my Dad,
just right for Father's Day.
I polished it
until it shone.
I hid it deep away.

When I gave it
to my Dad
he held it to his ear
and told me
I had given him
the whole, wide sea to hear.

Sandra Liatsos

Baby Animals (sung to "Mary Had a Little Lamb")

Sheep give birth to little lambs,
Little lambs, little lambs.
Sheep give birth to little lambs,
Yes, that's the baby's name.

Dogs and seals have little pups,
Little pups, little pups.
Dogs and seal have little pups,
Yes, that's the baby's name.

Cows and whales have little calves,
Little calves, little calves.
Cows and whales have little calves,
Yes, that's the baby's name.

Ostriches and hens have chicks,
Little chicks, little chicks.
Ostriches and hens have chicks,
Yes, that's the baby's name.

Bears and lions both have cubs,
Little cubs, little cubs.
Bears and lions both have cubs,
Yes, that's the baby's name.

Deer give birth to little fawns,
Little fawns, little fawns.
Deer give birth to little fawns,
Yes, that's the baby's name.

Antelope have little kids,
Little kids, little kids.
Antelope have little kids,
And people have kids, too!

Meish Goldish

Month-by-Month Poetry: March, April, May, June Scholastic Professional Books, 1999

Baby Chick

Peck
   peck
     peck
on the warm brown egg.
OUT comes a neck.
OUT comes a leg.

How
   does
     a chick
who's not been about,
discover the trick
of how to get out?

Aileen Fisher

Farm Riddle

Peep, Peep, Peep!
It's morning on the farm.
Who's that waking up, up, up
Inside the big red barn?

Answer: It's a chick!

Cornelia Parsons

Note: To change the riddle, replace line one with other farm animal sounds such as "Cock-a-doodle-do," "Baah, baah, baah!" or "Moo, moo, moo!".

The Chickens

Said the first little chicken
With a queer little squirm:
"I wish I could find
A fat little worm!"

Said the next little chicken,
With an odd little shrug:
"I wish I could find
A fat little bug!"

Said the third little chicken,
With a small sigh of grief:
"I wish I could find
A green little leaf!"

Said the fourth little chicken,
With a faint little moan:
"I wish I could find
A wee gravel stone!"

"Now see here!" said the mother,
From the green garden patch,
"If you want any breakfast,
Just come here and scratch!"

Anonymous

Month-by-Month Poetry: March, April, May, June Scholastic Professional Books, 1999

Frog

A frog once went out walking,
In the pleasant summer air,
He happened into a barber's shop
And skipped into the chair.
The barber said in disbelief;
"Your brains are surely bare.
How can you have a haircut
When you haven't any hair?"

Anonymous

Frog Song

On a lily-pad throne,
You float like a king.
Then when it gets dusky,
You start to sing:
Ribbity ribbit croakity croak,
Ribbity ribbit croakity croak—
I love every sandpaper note!

Liza Charlesworth

School

When school lets out in June, I feel
    As happy as can be.
I hop and skip and jump and run
    And shout and laugh with glee.
I'm sure that I will never want
    To go to school again,
But when September comes around,
    I always like to then.

Iva Riebel Judy

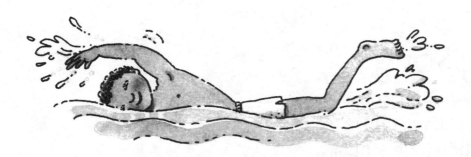

The Lesson

I splash—I flop,
I tread—I hop,
My arms go in a spin
My legs are kicking up and down
Then—suddenly! I swim.

Jane W. Krows

Month-by-Month Poetry: March, April, May, June Scholastic Professional Books, 1999

Summer

Rushes in a watery place,
    And reeds in a hollow;
A soaring skylark in the sky,
    A darting swallow;
And where pale blossom used to hang
    Ripe fruit to follow.

Christina Rossetti

Smells of Summer

There are certain things in summer
That smell real nice to me.
The moss and ferns and woodsy things
I like especially.

The grassy lawn just freshly cut,
The fragrant stacks of hay,
The clean outdoors when it has rained,
The salty ocean spray—

Pine needles warming in the sun,
Fresh corn, and berries, too,
Bright flowers in a big bouquet—
I like these smells, don't you?

Vivian Gouled

Autograph Verse

Read	see	that	me
up	will	I	like
and	you	like	you
down	and	you	if

Anonymous

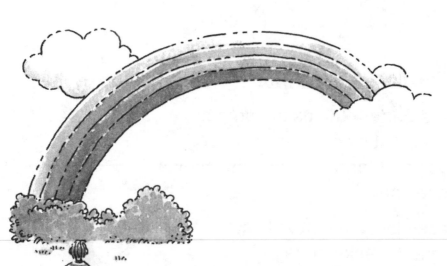

The Rainbow

The rainbow's like a colored bridge
that sometimes shines from ridge to ridge.
Today one end is in the sea,
the other's in this field with me.

Iain Crichton-Smith

Notes

Month-by-Month Poetry: March, April, May, June Scholastic Professional Books, 1999

Notes

Month-by-Month Poetry: March, April, May, June Scholastic Professional Books, 1999